GW00383851

Flavours of Wales

THE WELSH CAKE COOKBOOK

Gilli Davies and Huw Jones

GRAFFEG

The Welsh Cake Cookbook
Published in Great Britain in 2016 by
Graffeg Limited

Text by Gilli Davies copyright © 2016.
Photographs by Huw Jones copyright © 2016.
Food styling by André Moore.
Designed and produced by Graffeg Limited
copyright © 2016

Graffeg Limited, 24 Stradey Park Business
Centre, Mwrwg Road, Llangennech, Llanelli,
Carmarthenshire SA14 8YP Wales UK
Tel 01554 824000 www.graffeg.com

Gilli Davies is hereby identified as the author of
this work in accordance with section 77 of the
Copyrights, Designs and Patents Act 1988.

A CIP Catalogue record for this book is
available from the British Library.

All rights reserved. No part of this publication
may be reproduced, stored in a retrieval system
or transmitted, in any form or by any means,
electronic, mechanical, photocopying, recording
or otherwise, without the prior permission of
the publishers.

ISBN 9781910862025

1 2 3 4 5 6 7 8 9

CONTENTS

Welsh Cakes

Hot off the griddle, rich, moist, crumble and moreish, these little cakes are so well loved in Wales, they could become the national emblem.

Visit any market or food festival and you will catch the scent of freshly griddled Welsh cakes wafting in the air. Just walk past a bakery where they are being prepared, and you will find it hard not to dive in and buy some.

Welsh cakes are peculiar to Wales, for although other Celtic countries use the griddle for baking – the Irish with their famous potato cakes, the Scots with their oatcakes and the Bretonnes with their crepes – none make a sweet scone-like delicacy with quite the same appeal as the Welsh cake.

Hospitality is part of the Welsh nature and the people of Wales love to share their food. It's a thing from the past. Making and giving food to friends and visitors stems from harder times when the small rural communities would support each other in times of need. It's no wonder then that the Welsh cake has always been a firm favourite throughout Wales. With the ingredients of flour, butter, eggs and milk easy to obtain in a rural setting, when they could be bartered or exchanged for perhaps some fresh vegetables, or soft fruit.

In particular, Welsh cakes have been tea-time favourites in south Wales since the latter part of the 18th century. At one time they would have been eaten regularly in the larger farmhouses and smaller cottages alike. And miners would also expect to find them in their food-boxes. Originally they were cooked either on the griddle over the open fire or in what was known as a Dutch Oven, which was a small metal container which was placed in front of the fire or in the warm ashes. The Welsh names for Welsh cakes are Pice ar y Maen or Cacen Gri, which are based on the Welsh name for the griddle or bakestone.

How to prepare Welsh cakes – basic principles

Either use a food processor or mixer to prepare the Welsh cakes. Alternatively you could simply rub the mixture together with your fingertips, but use a large bowl and lift your cool hands high out of the bowl to stop the butter getting too warm and making the mixture very sticky. Once the butter has been well mixed into the flour and the other ingredients have been added, press the mixture together fairly quickly and transfer to a cool worktop or board. Using a minimal amount of flour, roll or press the dough out into a large circle so that it is about 1cm thick.

Cut to the required shape and size, usually about 6cm diameter, but it could be cocktail size or as big as a dinner plate, and griddle as soon as you can, so that the raising agent in the flour has maximum effect and makes the Welsh cakes as light as possible. Either use a traditional solid iron bakestone, which may need to be oiled, or a large non-stick frying pan. The Welsh cakes are rich enough not to need any extra oil or butter when cooking, but they do benefit from a fine dusting of caster sugar while still hot after griddling.

TRADITIONAL
WELSH CAKES

There is nothing more to say about these delightful little griddle cakes, except that they are exceptionally moreish!

TRADITIONAL WELSH CAKES

Ingredients

225g self-raising flour

100g butter or a mixture of butter and lard

75g caster sugar

75g currants

½ teaspoon mixed spice

1 teaspoon honey

1 medium egg, beaten

1 In a bowl, rub the fats into the flour until the mixture resembles breadcrumbs.

2 Stir in the sugar, currants, mixed spice and honey.

3 Add the beaten egg and mix to form a firm dough.

4 On a floured board, roll or pat out the mixture until about 1cm thick and cut into 6cm discs.

5 Heat a griddle or large frying pan to a medium heat and griddle gently until golden brown on both sides (only grease the griddle if you think the Welsh cakes will stick).

6 Dust the Welsh cakes with caster sugar and eat immediately, or store in an airtight tin.

TINKERS'
CAKE

These scrumptious cakes were originally made when the tinker was doing his rounds. Prepared and griddled in a matter of minutes, hopefully they would tempt the tinker to offer a bargain or two.

TINKERS' CAKE

Ingredients

225g self-raising flour

100g butter or a mixture of butter and lard

75g demerara sugar

1 large cooking apple, peeled, cored and grated

1 small egg, beaten

1 Rub the butter, or mixed fats, into the flour until the mixture resembles breadcrumbs.

2 Add the sugar, apple and beaten egg to make a soft dough.

On a floured board, either:

3 Roll or pat the dough out until about 1cm thick and cut into discs.

4 Or divide the dough and roll out into two largish circles.

5 Griddle over moderate heat for 4-5 minutes on each side, taking care when turning the large discs.

6 Sprinkle with caster sugar and cut the large tinkers' cakes into wedges to serve.

HEART-SHAPED LAVENDER WELSH CAKES

I first made these fragrant recipes for a local lavender farm where they went down a treat. If lavender is supposed to have relaxing qualities, then I suggest you nibble one or two at bedtime to guarantee a good night's sleep.

HEART-SHAPED LAVENDER WELSH CAKES

Ingredients

225g self-raising flour

100g mixed butter and lard

75g caster sugar

1 teaspoon crushed lavender flowers

1 teaspoon honey

1 medium egg, beaten

1 In a bowl, rub the fats into the flour until the mixture resembles breadcrumbs.

2 Stir in the sugar, lavender and honey.

3 Add the beaten egg and mix to form a firm dough.

4 On a floured board, roll or pat out the mixture until about 1cm thick and cut into heart shapes.

5 Heat a griddle or large frying pan to a medium heat and griddle gently until golden brown on both sides (only grease the griddle if you think they will stick).

6 Dust the lavender Welsh cakes with caster sugar while still warm.

APPLE AND BLACKBERRY WELSH CAKE SPLITS

APPLE AND BLACKBERRY WELSH CAKE SPLITS

Ingredients

225g self-raising flour

100g butter or a mixture of butter and lard

75g caster sugar

75g currants

½ teaspoon mixed spice

1 teaspoon honey

1 medium egg, beaten

Apple Cheese

2 cooking apples, peeled, cored and chopped roughly

25g butter

2 tablespoons water

25g caster sugar

Pinch of nutmeg

Stew the apples with the other ingredients until you have a firm purée.

Blackberry Sauce

A good cupful of blackberries

2 tablespoons water

25g caster sugar

A small glass of Cassis blackcurrant liqueur (optional)

Stew the blackberries with the other ingredients until soft then sieve to make a purée.

1 In a bowl, rub the butter or the mixed fats into into the flour until the mixture resembles breadcrumbs.

2 Stir in the sugar, currants, mixed spice and honey.

3 Add the beaten egg and mix to form a firm dough.

4 On a floured board, roll the mixture until about 1cm thick and cut into 6cm discs.

5 Heat a griddle or large frying pan to a medium heat and griddle gently until golden brown on both sides.

6 **To Serve:** Split the Welsh cakes, fill with some apple and surround with the blackberry purée.

These Welsh cakes have an authentic autumn flavour and I always think that blackberries gathered from the hedgerow taste the best.

HAZELNUT AND TREACLE WELSH CAKES

Hazelnuts and treacle are a match made in heaven, so why not pack some up for your next outdoor adventure - a walk in Snowdonia or a trip to Swansea Bay.

HAZELNUT AND TREACLE WELSH CAKES

Ingredients

225g self-raising flour

100g butter or a mixture of butter and lard

75g caster sugar

75g hazelnuts, roasted, shelled and chopped

1 teaspoon black treacle

1 egg, beaten

1 In a bowl, rub the fats into the flour until the mixture resembles breadcrumbs.

2 Stir in the sugar, nuts and treacle.

3 Add the beaten egg and mix to form a firm dough.

4 On a floured board, roll or pat out the mixture until about 1cm thick and cut into discs.

5 Heat a griddle or large frying pan to a medium heat and griddle gently until golden brown on both sides. Dust with caster sugar while still warm.

CRANBERRY AND WHITE CHOCOLATE WELSH CAKES

These particular Welsh cakes stay really moist with the addition of cranberries, and white chocolate just adds to the deliciousness.

CRANBERRY AND WHITE CHOCOLATE WELSH CAKES

Ingredients

225g self-raising flour

100g mixed butter and lard

75g dried cranberries

50g white chocolate chips

25g caster sugar

1 egg, beaten

1. In a bowl, rub the fats into the flour until the mixture resembles breadcrumbs.

2. Stir in the cranberries, white chocolate chips and sugar.

3. Add the beaten egg and mix to form a firm dough.

4. On a floured board, roll or pat out the mixture until about 1cm thick and cut into discs.

5. Heat a griddle or large frying pan to a medium heat and griddle gently until golden brown on both sides.

6. Dust the Welsh cakes with caster sugar and eat immediately, or store in an airtight tin.

DOUBLE CHOCOLATE CHIP WELSH CAKES

Welsh cakes designed for the younger nibbler and recommended for chocoholics.

DOUBLE CHOCOLATE CHIP WELSH CAKES

Ingredients

225g self-raising flour

100g butter or a mixture of butter and lard

50g dark chocolate chips

50g milk chocolate chips

A couple of drops of vanilla essence

1 medium egg, beaten

1 In a bowl, rub the butter into the flour until the mixture resembles breadcrumbs.

2 Stir in the chocolate chips and vanilla.

3 Add the beaten egg and mix to form a firm dough.

4 On a floured board, roll or pat out the mixture until about 1cm thick and cut into discs. I like to use a gingerbread man cutter when cooking these for children.

5 Heat a griddle or large frying pan to a medium heat and griddle gently until golden brown on both sides. Take care not to burn yourself if the chocolate chips start to melt.

6 Dust the Welsh cakes with caster sugar and eat immediately, or store in an airtight tin.

CAERPHILLY CHEESE AND LEEK WELSH CAKES

The best of flavours in these savoury Welsh cakes, they would be perfect to nibble with a glass of Welsh white wine.

CAERPHILLY CHEESE AND LEEK WELSH CAKES

Ingredients

1 medium leek, washed and finely shredded

50g Caerphilly cheese, grated

225g self-raising flour

50g butter

1 small egg, beaten

1 Dunk the leek in boiling water for 5 minutes then rinse under the cold tap and squeeze dry.

2 In a bowl, rub the butter into the flour until the mixture resembles breadcrumbs.

3 Stir in cooled cooked leek and grated cheese.

4 Add the beaten egg and mix to form a firm dough.

5 On a floured board, roll or pat out the mixture until about 1cm thick and cut into discs.

6 Heat a griddle or large frying pan to a medium heat and griddle gently until golden brown on both sides (only grease the griddle if you think the Welsh cakes will stick).

BACON AND GOUDA
WELSH CAKES

John Savage makes an excellent Gouda cheese in Carmarthenshire and it has inspired me to create these savoury Welsh cakes.

BACON AND GOUDA WELSH CAKES

Ingredients

4 rashers streaky bacon, rinded and diced

50g mature Gouda cheese, grated

225g self-raising flour

100g butter or a mixture of butter and lard

1 large egg, beaten

1 Dry fry the diced bacon in a frying pan with no added fat until it is crispy, then cool.

2 In a bowl, rub the butter into the flour until the mixture resembles breadcrumbs.

3 Stir in the bacon and grated cheese.

4 Add the beaten egg and mix to form a firm dough.

5 On a floured board, roll or pat out the mixture until about 1cm thick and cut into discs.

6 Heat a griddle or large frying pan to a medium heat and griddle gently until golden brown on both sides (only grease the griddle if you think the Welsh cakes will stick).

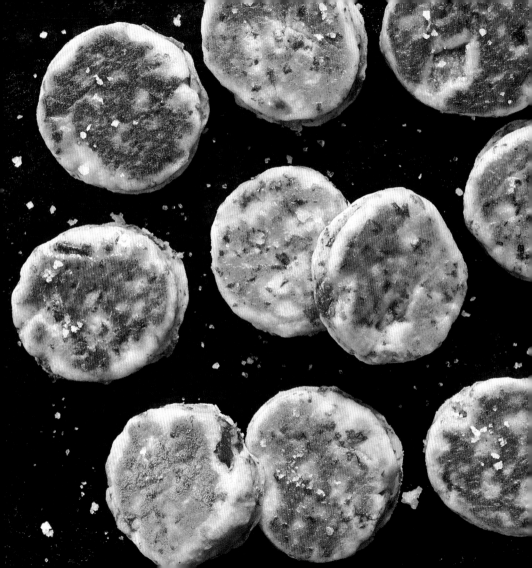

LAVERBREAD AND BACON WELSH CAKES

Surely this is the perfect Welsh breakfast Welsh cake including the tradional ingredients of laverbread and bacon. Why not finish the effect with some cockles and creamy scrambled eggs?

LAVERBREAD AND BACON WELSH CAKES

Ingredients

4 rashers streaky bacon, rinded and diced

2 tablespoons pulped laverbread

225g self-raising flour

100g butter or a mixture of butter and lard

1 medium egg, beaten

1. Dry fry the diced bacon in a frying pan with no added fat until it is crispy, then cool.

2. In a bowl, rub the butter into the flour until the mixture resembles breadcrumbs.

3. Stir in the diced bacon and laverbread.

4. Add the beaten egg and mix to form a soft dough.

5. On a floured board, roll or pat out the mixture until about 1cm thick and cut into discs.

6. Heat a griddle or large frying pan to a medium heat and griddle gently until golden brown on both sides. (Only grease the griddle if you think the Welsh cakes will stick).

METRIC AND IMPERIAL EQUIVALENTS

Weights	Solid		Volume	Liquid
15g	½oz		15ml	½ floz
25g	1oz		30ml	1 floz
40g	1½oz		50ml	2 floz
50g	1¾oz		100ml	3½ floz
75g	2¾oz		125ml	4 floz
100g	3½oz		150ml	5 floz (¼ pint)
125g	4½oz		200ml	7 floz
150g	5½oz		250ml	9 floz
175g	6oz		300ml	10 floz (½ pint)
200g	7oz		400ml	14 floz
250g	9oz		450ml	16 floz
300g	10½oz		500ml	18 floz
400g	14oz		600ml	1 pint (20 floz)
500g	1lb 2oz		1 litre	1¾ pints
1kg	2lb 4oz		1.2 litre	2 pints
1.5kg	3lb 5oz		1.5 litre	2¾ pints
2kg	4lb 8oz		2 litres	3½ pints
3kg	6lb 8oz		3 litres	5¼ pints

WELSH COOKBOOKS
GILLI DAVIES AND HUW JONES

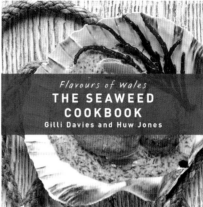

Gilli Davies does it again with three new cookbooks featuring Welsh Cakes, Seaweed and Sea Salt recipes.

Flavours of Wales Cookbooks make wonderful gifts £6.99.

Available from all good bookshops, kitchen and gift shops and online www.graffeg.com Tel 01554 824000.

GRAFFEG
Books and Gifts from Wales

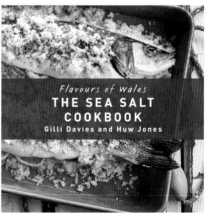

FLAVOURS OF WALES COLLECTION

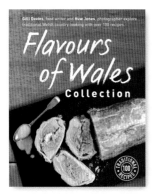

Cook up a Welsh feast with the full *Flavours of Wales* collection in cookbooks, pocket books and notecards to share with friends.

Flavours of Wales Collection book with over 100 recipes by Gilli Davies, photographed by Huw Jones £20.00

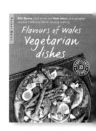

10 Recipe Notecards and envelopes in a gift pack. Full recipe inside with space for a message £8.99

Flavours of Wales Collection in a gift slip case with 5 pock books £12.99

Flavours of Wales pocket books £2.99

Available from all good bookshops, kitchen and gift shops and online www.graffeg.com Tel 01554 824000.

GRAFFEG
Books and Gifts from Wales